PROOFS
OF HIS
PRESENCE

PROOFS OF HIS PRESENCE

Grace Noll Crowell

ABINGDON PRESS

NEW YORK
NASHVILLE

PROOFS OF HIS PRESENCE

Copyright © 1958 by Abingdon Press

Library of Congress Catalog Card Number: 58-10455

"O Gracious, Mighty Shepherd," "Church Spires," and
"The Migrant Worker" are from *Lutheran Herald;* "Our
Dwelling Place" and "My Bible," from *Church in the Home,*
are copyright 1956 by Pilgrim Press; "The Master Teacher,"
from *Church in the Home,* is copyright 1957 by Pilgrim Press;
"Withheld Knowledge," from *Church in the Home,* is copy-
right 1958 by Pilgrim Press; "The Final Triumph" is from
The Herald of Holiness; "This Is the Book," from *Home,* is
copyright 1955 by Judson Press; "The Lord Is in His Holy
Temple," from *Wesley Quarterly,* is copyright 1956 by The
Methodist Publishing House; "I Heard the World at Prayer"
is copyright 1955 by Prayer Life Movement; "That by Which
We Live" is copyright 1955 by *The War Cry.*

PRINTED AND BOUND AT NASHVILLE,
TENNESSEE, UNITED STATES OF AMERICA

THIS BOOK IS AFFECTIONATELY DEDICATED

to all true believers in the risen Christ:
the One infinitely loving and wise,
who has given us many infallible proofs
of his immortality, and of our own.

It is dedicated to those who receive
these proofs with unshakable faith,
and with heartfelt gratitude for the
light his revelations shed upon our upward and onward way.

FOREWORD

IF SOME BEWILDERED ONE, FALTERING upon his heavenward journey, should find help in these simple portrayals of Christ's living presence after his resurrection, and of his vital meaning in our lives today, I shall be forever grateful.

Should some word herein prove thus helpful, it will only be because, through prayer for wisdom, the Lord has permitted me to be a humble spokesman.

GRACE NOLL CROWELL

CONTENTS

PROOFS
OF HIS
PRESENCE

My Bible

I have this library of important books—
It is encompassed in a narrow space,
But one can find within it if one looks
The mighty saga of the human race.
I am rich—I own the history of time.
I have access to the wisdom that God speaks.
Through it I have the impetus to climb
Beyond earth's hills to heaven's highest peaks.

I own the map of ages as I go
Certain of my charted destiny,
Following the outlaid course, I know
I shall arrive—as I scan earnestly
The footprints of man's march across the sod
Toward the everlasting citadels of God.

1. HE IS RISEN

> The former treatise have I made, O
> Theophilus, of all that Jesus began both
> to do and teach, until the day in which
> he was taken up, after that he through
> the Holy Ghost had given command-
> ments unto the apostles whom he had
> chosen: to whom also he shewed him-
> self alive after his passion by many in-
> fallible proofs.
>
> Acts 1:1-3

H E IS RISEN!" THREE BRIEF WORDS, YET THEY CARRY
enough meaning and power to lift this
heavily weighted world out of darkness into
light.

They are like three clear-struck gong notes that
have sounded across earth's darkest valleys. They
have leapt from mountain peak to mountain peak,
leaving a reverberating silver sound throughout the
centuries, and still they go echoing on and on, and
will be giving out their message of hope throughout
time and eternity.

"He is risen!" When the cry first rang out across
an ancient garden, it was difficult, indeed, for Christ's
followers to believe the soul-shaking news.

Their hearts had been so torn, so numbed, by the
great tragedy that they apparently had forgotten his
promise to be with them again.

The Christ was dead and buried. They had witnessed it all. Some had been close enough to his cross to hear the dull, sickening hammer blows on feet and hands. One had stood so near him that he was able to catch the last gentle command Christ uttered in behalf of his precious mother.

They had followed the procession which wound its way down the hillside, and on into the Gethsemane garden. They had seen the body laid tenderly away in the new tomb of Joseph of Arimathea. Their friend was gone from them, and all that was left for them now was cruel disappointment and the bleakest sorrow, so they felt.

Now it was being offered to them in three brief words, the clear proof of his immortality—of yours and of mine—yet they were unable to receive it, or to believe it, so difficult it was for them to comprehend that stupendous truth.

It is sad, indeed, to know that their friend felt it necessary to remain on earth full forty days before taking his upward departure into the glory awaiting him there with his Father. Forty more days of tramping the roughened roadways of the world, waiting to waken their faith and to stir their hurt hearts into gladness once more, and he lingered on, finally accomplishing his purpose with them, and with us, his followers of today.

"He is risen!" This is the message of triumph that will be shouted out throughout the ages. It will be sung by great cathedral choirs. It will be repeated over and over by groping, suffering humanity until

14

its meaning is clear and steadfast in their hearts. It will prove to be a certainty of entrance into heaven for all true believers.

"He is risen!" Our friend—our hunger-satisfying, thirst-quenching Saviour—is risen, as he said. We thank thee, God.

Our blessed Lord, we are grateful for the unchanging truth of thy Word, for thy companionship here on earth, and for the hope that thou hast given us, that we, if we but believe, can and will spend eternity in thy presence. AMEN.

"Because I Live"

Christ said: "Because I live, ye shall live also."
O men, lay hold upon his blessed Word.
This is our hope, like some high lifted banner
Unfurled against the sky. Our hearts have heard
No clearer message, and no truer music,
Than this assurance from the Christ's own
    tongue—
Because he lives, he says, we shall live also,
Forever joyous, and forever young.

Forever to advance in greater knowledge,
To fully know the truth that sets us free,
To walk companioned by the living Saviour
Throughout the reaches of eternity—
Oh, what more blessed news could we be hear-
    ing
Than these words loosed upon the winds of
    time?
They lie ahead of us—the hills of heaven—
With him for comrade, and with strength to
    climb.

2. MARY MAGDALENE

> The first day of the week cometh Mary
> Magdalene . . . unto the sepulchre.
>
> John 20:1

*E*VIDENTLY MARY MAGDALENE WAS A BEAUTIFUL
woman. The devil had tortured her greatly,
a torment that is not always inflicted upon
her plainer sisters. His hatred of the Christ is so
fierce, so unrelenting, that he ever strives to hurt any
one of the Lord's children upon whom he can wield
his evil influence, and Mary was one of his victims.
She had indeed been a great sufferer beneath his
ruthless hands.

Then one blessed day she met the Lord, and he
freed her from her cruel bondage. Her inner life
was immediately turned from darkness into light.
The serenity of her countenance bore testimony to
the change that had taken place within her, and she
was ever afterward one of Christ's most devout followers and worshipers.

She owed her Lord a great debt and she felt she
could repay him a portion of that debt in a last sad
rite. Thus, to anoint his precious body, she brought
in her arms all the sweetness she could gather of
earth's fragrant spices. She came slowly through the
dew-wet garden, trailing her dark robes against the
leaning bushes. A heady fragrance followed her

along the pathway as she moved. The waking birds, startled by her coming, gave forth a soft crooning sound.

She it was who first saw that the great stone had been rolled away from the door of the sepulchre, and she turned frantically back along the path, meeting Peter and John, who were entering the garden. She cried out as she went: "They have taken away the Lord out of the sepulchre, and we know not where they have laid him!"

The two men ran forward; John, outdistancing Peter, came to the tomb. They stopped and saw it was empty, that it was as Mary had said. They turned sadly homeward, not knowing as yet the scriptures, "that he must rise again from the dead."

But Mary stayed. She stood before the sepulchre weeping. No doubt she was shy, and much too humble, after her earlier experiences, to push herself forward into the sepulchre. But no heart was more loving, or more filled with gratitude, for her Lord and Saviour than was hers. She felt she would never be comforted again, never see the beauty about her, never rejoice in her own freedom from the evil influences that had so tortured her.

But, strangely, it was she who first saw the two angels, one at the head and one at the feet, where Jesus had lain. Matthew and Mark tell of but one angel, but Mary was given the privilege of seeing two of the glistening, white-robed ones who had come down from heaven to witness the momentous event of that springtime morning.

One of them spoke to her: "Woman, why weepest thou?" And Mary sobbed out her answer: "Because they have taken away my Lord, and I know not where they have laid him."

Small wonder that she was frightened and heartbroken at such a loss! Christ was her friend. He had loosed her from a hideous weight of evil. He had befriended her in countless ways. She had lost him by death, and she had mourned him with all her woman's heart; but to have his dear body taken away in some mysterious manner was too much to bear, and she stood weeping in the dawnlight.

She turned about, still bearing the sweet spices she had planned to use as her humble offering for him. There was One standing beside the pathway—evidently a stranger. Perhaps he is the gardener, she thought. He spoke to her: "Woman, why weepest thou? whom seekest thou?" And she answered through her tears: "Sir, if thou have borne him hence, tell me where thou hast laid him, and I will take him away." She would take him away! She was ready to undertake the impossible, so great was her love for her Lord.

And then a voice. Jesus spoke to her by name: "Mary," and she knew him! Oh the joy, the unspeakable joy of that moment! Can we not believe she flung herself prostrate at his feet as she uttered

19

his beloved name, "Rabboni," meaning he was her Master, and the Master of all mankind.

Two words—two names uttered there that morning as the dawn flooded the old garden with rose and silver light! Two names that hung trembling on the air, to be repeated over and over by countless millions as they have read, and will read to the end of time, of this beautiful reunion, this recognition of the woman for her Master, and his gentle voicing of her name.

To her life's end, Mary could testify of this proof given to her of the resurrection of the Christ. Even in this moment of excitement she did not fail to obey the command to "go tell my brethren."

Our beloved master and our Lord, we, too, would call out thy name in our great need for thee. In our own Gethsemanes on this earth we need to hear thy voice speaking our names, and we, too, would "go tell our brethren" of thy living, breathing presence. AMEN.

3. THE WALK TO EMMAUS

> And, behold, two of them went that
> same day to a village called Emmaus. . . .
> And they talked together of all these
> things which had happened.
>
> Luke 24:13-14

SPRING WAS NO DOUBT BURGEONING ON THE EMMAUS
road that day. Wild flowers swept the countryside with their vivid coloring, and the
birds were blithe and gay over the grassy meadowlands; but alas! the two who went their way were too
heavy of heart to take note of that glowing new life,
that clear, singing rapture.

How sad they were, these former believers in the
words of the Christ; How bowed down with grief!
Their conversation that day was of nothing and of
no one but their Lord—his words and his ways and
all that had happened.

Suddenly out of nowhere, it seemed, a stranger
joined them and walked by their side. His voice was
gentle, his eyes kind, his manner so gracious, that
they resented neither his coming nor his questioning.

"What manner of communications are these that
ye have one to another, as ye walk, and are sad?"

They looked at him with wonderment. Finally
Cleopas, who was walking next to him, answered:
"Art thou only a stranger in Jerusalem, and hast not

known the things which are come to pass there in these days?" And the stranger said unto them, "What things?"

No wonder his companions were astonished and bewildered, to think that anyone who had dwelt recently in the Jerusalem area should be ignorant of what had happened! They looked at him aghast, but "their eyes were holden," and they did not recognize their beloved friend and Saviour.

However, they could not help opening their hearts to him, this kindly but uninformed one, and they told him of their great bereavement. They had earnestly trusted that the Christ was to redeem Israel, but alas! it seemed now but a vague illusion, a spent dream.

What a pity—what a heartbreaking pity—that they could not say: "We trust, we are still trusting, that he will do as he said," not "we trusted." It would have been a great comfort to their companion on the road had he been assured of their steadfast faith, their unfaltering belief. It is blessed that he understands all our human frailties, our weakness and our instability. And so that day he walked on beside them, gravely and understandingly.

But when they spoke despairingly of the empty sepulcher, he said sternly: "O fools, and slow of heart to believe all that the prophets have spoken. Ought not Christ to have suffered these things, and to enter into his glory?" Then, beginning back in history, "he expounded unto them in all the scriptures the things concerning himself."

The men looked at him in astonishment. Here was one not so ignorant and uninformed after all. Here was one whose words caused their hearts to burn within them as they trod the long road that springtime day. Who on earth could he be, this wise one? Never had they met another like him.

They drew near at last to a little village—the home of Cleopas. The early evening light was streaming from the west across the small huddled huts. Here and there a star pricked its silver way through the deepening dusk; an occasional wick had been lighted in some earthen vessel and set upon a window sill to light the room, and the way for others.

They must be hospitable to this kindly stranger. Perhaps he was homeless and needed shelter for the night. Cleopas said to this strangely compelling personage, "Abide with us: for it is toward evening," and unhesitatingly he accepted the invitation.

Supper was ready and waiting in the room as they entered. The loaf of brown-crusted bread lay on the table. The flank of meat was ready to be carved. The good wife stood by, shyly smiling a welcome to their guest.

As a courtesy to the stranger, the host bade him break the bread. Slowly he reached for the loaf. They

23

noted that the hand had been recently wounded, but courtesy forbade their questioning him concerning it.

The stranger lifted his eyes heavenward and asked God's blessing upon the little household. He gave thanks for the food, and then, and only then, they recognized him! It was Jesus, their beloved Lord! Oh, the miracle of it! Oh, the longing to detain him, to have him further expound the scriptures for the little family gathered about the board. But he was gone—vanished as he had appeared.

The men did not wait for their supper. All the weariness from the long walk had vanished, and they returned that same night to Jerusalem. There they joined the eleven, who were gathered together in hushed expectancy.

The two entered the room, crying aloud their joyful news. "The Lord is risen—he is risen indeed! He walked and talked with us on the way. He is as vitally alive as he was before his crucifixion. Praise be to his name!"

Among the many infallible proofs of Christ's resurrection, this event is one of the most precious in its meaning to mankind. It has a home-sweet setting for all who count him ever as a gracious household guest, for all who live by his word, and who bow their heads above their daily bread. Let us rejoice that the Christ is alive today as he was then. Let us praise his holy name.

Our blessed Lord, we, too, bid thee abide with us, the families of the earth. Make our dwellings thy resting place, our food thy food, our fire thy warmth. We would honor thee above all guests. We are grateful for thy presence. AMEN.

4. THE ELEVEN

> And they rose up the same hour, and
> returned to Jerusalem, and found the
> eleven gathered together.
>
> Luke 24:33

THERE IS SOMETHING SAD ABOUT THIS PARTICULAR
number: eleven. There should have been
twelve ardent and earnest followers of the
Christ, but one had committed the blackest crime of
all history and had gone out into utter darkness, to
return no more. But among the eleven gathered together in one room, there was a spirit of reverence.
To delight their hearts and strengthen their faith,
they were soon to have unquestionable proof of the
Christ's resurrection.

There was a sudden commotion at the door as
Simon and Cleopas entered. They were breathless
from their long walk from Emmaus, and almost too
excited to speak; but they managed at length to im-
part the marvelous news: they had walked and
talked with the risen Lord that very afternoon. With
what eagerness was this news received!

The questions came all too fast for answering:
How did he look? What did he say? Shall we, too,
see him?

Then suddenly a movement, a stirring as if the
wind had blown against the door—it opened, and

the Christ entered the room. The men stood spellbound. This could not be the Christ in person! It must be his spirit, or would they not have heard his footsteps at the door, or have seen him entering? Their thoughts had been so intent upon him that they were sure this was but an apparition.

Then came the well-known, well-loved voice: "Peace be unto you." This was the salutation customary among the Jewish people. It means, "May you prosper in body and soul, and enjoy every heavenly and earthly good."

Despite their doubting minds, Jesus stood in their midst. He had come to remove that doubt. He was with them again. It is ever thus. "Where two or three are gathered together in my name," he says, "there am I in the midst of them."

Still he found them difficult to convince. "Handle me and see. A spirit hath not flesh and bones as ye see me have," he explained.

They drew near to him—they touched his outstretched hands; they bowed down at his sandaled feet. It was the Lord! They knew him at last.

He was hungry, even as they grew hungry after a long walk in the open. They offered him a bit of broiled fish; they saw him taste appreciatively of the honey set before him, and their hearts were overflowing with a great joy.

Then and there, standing in their midst, "he opened their understanding, that they might understand the scriptures." What a revelation it must have been to them! How enlightened were the corners of their darkened minds!

He alone can illuminate the Word of God for humanity. Without the light of Christ's teachings, the Bible would be a closed book to men's minds and hearts.

That night the Lord revealed many things to his eager listeners. He told them of work ahead waiting to be done: work which they alone could do, that others might be brought into the knowledge so needed to evangelize the world. They were to be his witnesses, and he bade them to begin the work there in Jerusalem. They were to work among his murderers, making overtures there, telling these men of Christ's mercy and forgiveness, that these evil ones might repent and be saved. His last command that evening was that they were to tarry in Jerusalem until they were "endued with power from on high," which they did.

What a glorious hour that must have been for the eleven! They had witnessed a miracle. They had their Friend back with them for a season, and they were joyful at the thought of going forth to do his bidding.

Forty days were to elapse—days in which doubtless they would occasionally be permitted to walk and talk with their Master, to learn more of the duties required of them. Then one fair summer day they went with him on a last long walk into the country. There are several authorities who disagree upon their destination. Luke says, "He led them

28

out as far as to Bethany," a village about fifteen furlongs from Jerusalem. Another says they went to Mount Olivet, which is a "sabbath day's journey" from their starting point.

At any rate it no doubt was a beautiful, cloudless day, and the walk must have been pleasant, especially so to Jesus, whose stay on earth was over and who knew whither he was going.

Doubtless the eleven knew it was their last hour with him, but their hearts were no longer saddened. They understood the meaning of Christ's earthly pilgrimage. They knew they could trust whatever he did as being wise for them and for their good. He had given them the most convincing proof of his friendship, and his work was finished.

They stopped in the cool green countryside—probably in the midst of a wind-blown meadow. He must have spoken lovingly to each of his friends, and he lifted up his hands and blessed them, putting a hand on each forehead, which seems to have been the form of paternal blessing in those days.

Oh, to have been one among them that day! To have seen him slowly, safely lifting upward, drawn by some unseen power! To have seen the sunlight glinting on his hair, the gentle wind blowing his garments, as up and up and up he went, until the blue illimitable sky itself received him and bore him forever from their sight!

We are told that the watchers fell on their knees in worship there beneath the empty sky, and they returned to Jerusalem to be his ardent witnesses, a great joy welling in their hearts. Their Lord lived, and would live for evermore! He had gone to prepare a place for them, and they could await his bidding.

Heavenly Father, it is good to think of thy reunion with thy Son that far-off day. May we so revere him and serve him that we, too, may find a joyous welcome in the place that thou hast prepared for all those who love thee and serve thee aright. AMEN.

Our Dwelling Place
(Ps. 90:1-2)

"Lord, thou hast been our dwelling place
For all generations." Thou wert God
Before the earth was hurled through boundless
    space,
Or humanity walked freely on its sod;
Before the mountains had leapt skyward, or the
    seas
Came roaring in upon some lengthened shore.
Lord, thou hast been our dwelling place, and
    these
Thy works will praise thy name for evermore.

"From everlasting thou art God," and we
Can claim thee as our own. O blessed Lord,
"Appear unto thy servants," may there be
For us, and for our children, the award
Of thy great glory, like the light of day
To guide us safely on our heavenward way.

5. STEPHEN

> And Stephen, full of faith and power, did great wonders and miracles among the people.
>
> Acts 6:8

THE EXPERIENCE OF MARTYRED STEPHEN IS TRULY one of the outstanding proofs of a living Christ.

Although Christ had gone from the earth in bodily form, he kept his promise and sent the Holy Ghost to the hearts of all those who would receive him and believe on him, and Stephen was one of the believers.

"Stephen, a man full of faith and of the Holy Ghost," we read, and further proof is brought clearly to mind upon his last hour on earth as he died beneath the cruel, ruthless hands of his murderers. In their rage at his words they were "cut to the heart," and they "gnashed on him with their teeth." His accusations of their wild and evil lives were all too true, and they sought a vicious revenge.

But Stephen, "full of the Holy Ghost, looked up stedfastly unto heaven, and saw the glory of God, and Jesus standing on the right hand of God, and said, Behold, I see the heavens opened, and the Son of man standing on the right hand of God."

This was the first time, after his ascension, that Jesus was seen of man, and Stephen was the privileged one. What a ringing testimony of a living Christ!

They killed Stephen, of course, even as they had killed Christ before him, but they could not kill the indwelling spirit. They could not destroy his faith in a living Saviour. It was directly to Christ that Stephen cried, "Lord Jesus, receive my spirit"; and with a loud voice, so that the last man at the throng's edge could not fail to hear him, he cried again, "Lord, lay not this sin to their charge." Then his spotless spirit was freed from his tortured body, to take its heavenward way.

How Christlike was Stephen! What a replica he was of the man on the cross! His last words were the words of the Christ. Crystal-clear they sound down the ages as an example of Christian forbearance. How pleasing must the man Stephen be to Christ!

We reread the words: "Jesus standing on the right hand of God," standing as a mediator between God and man. It was thus Stephen beheld him. Thank God that he still stands there in your behalf and mine, ready to receive all who call upon his name.

Adam Clarke's Commentary declares: "Here is a most manifest proof that *prayer is offered to Jesus Christ*; and that in the most solemn circumstances in which it could be offered, viz., when a man was *breathing his last.*" Then he goes on to say:

"This is, properly speaking, one of the *highest acts of worship* which can be offered to God; and, if Stephen had not conceived Jesus Christ to be God, could he have committed his soul into his hands?"

God and Jesus Christ are truly one, and there is the creed of millions:

I believe in God, the Father Almighty, Maker of heaven and earth; and in Jesus Christ, His only Son our Lord; who was conceived by the Holy Spirit, born of the Virgin Mary, suffered under Pontius Pilate, was crucified, dead, and buried; the third day, He rose from the dead; . . . and sitteth at the right hand of God the Father Almighty . . .

even as witnessed by Stephen, with his shining faith and his unwavering trust in his, and our, Lord.

Heavenly Father, we thank thee for proof of the everlasting existence of thy Son, Jesus Christ, for the fellowship he has with thee, and for his saving power for all men.

We thank thee that thou art God, maker of all things, ruler over lands and seas, and that thou art a just and merciful God. AMEN.

6. A CHOSEN VESSEL

> And Saul, yet breathing out threaten-
> ings and slaughter against the disciples of
> the Lord, went unto the high priest. . . .
> And as he journeyed, he came near Da-
> mascus: and suddenly there shined
> round about him a light from heaven:
> and he fell to the earth, and heard a
> voice saying unto him, Saul, Saul, why
> persecutest thou me?
>
> Acts 9:1-4

THAT VOICE WAS THE VOICE OF THE LORD, AND
here is the second proof given to man, after
the Ascension, concerning the Saviour's living presence.

Strange it is, indeed, that anyone as evil as Saul
apparently was, should thus be favored, thus singled
out as a chosen vessel of the Lord! But the Lord
knew the man. He knew that, in all of Saul's zeal-
ous attempts to destroy the infant church, this man
felt in his heart he was "doing God's service."
He knew Saul's great possibilities for future use-
fulness in the Kingdom, if his aims were directed
in the right channel. And later on, Paul the evangelist did not disappoint his Saviour.

Some have said that the great white light that
felled the man to earth was the brilliant electricity
of lightning, so controlled by the hand of God that

it would not prove fatal, although it was bright enough to blind Saul completely for a season.

Instead of this explanation, we might well be inclined to believe that the light was the glistening glory of the Christ himself shining around and about this journeying one. We recall that, after his heavenly contacts, even Moses' face glowed. How much more light would the Christ bring down from the glory land than would any earthly visitor!

Beneath this intense light, Saul fell to the earth, and lying prone, he cried: "Who art thou, Lord?" And the answer came: "Saul, Saul, why persecutest thou me? . . . I am Jesus whom thou persecutest: it is hard for thee to kick against the pricks."

In olden days a man driving a team of oxen carried a long stick with a sharpened iron point fastened at the end, with which he prodded his team forward. Often a stubborn ox would kick back violently against the goad, thus receiving more hurt to himself than he would from the relatively gentle prodding of the driver.

The prick that Jesus referred to must have, in a way of speaking, been that sort of goad. Surely Saul had kicked back against anything that was striving to direct him into the forward and right direction. Trembling under the strong apprehension of meeting the punishment he deserved, he questioned: "Lord, what wilt thou have me to do?"

The white light about him must have illuminated the very depths of his soul, or the man Saul would not have uttered that humble query so foreign to his nature.

The men who were with him stood aside, amazed and speechless, hearing a voice but seeing no man, and unable to distinguish the spoken words.

They saw Saul staggering to his feet, and they knew by his strange groping that he was totally blind. It must, indeed, have been one of the most dramatic moments in history: before them was their dauntless leader, the burning-eyed zealot groping helplessly for a hand to lead him, ashen-faced from his recent strange experience.

No change of character in anyone has been more marvelous, more complete, than that in Saul. The Lord chose him, then and there, because of the great possibilities that lay dormant in the man for future service in the Kingdom.

Paul the evangelist! His words echo down the ages, as true and vital today as when they were uttered. The throngs followed him and became believers. Ever "he spake boldly in the name of the Lord Jesus." (Acts 9:29.)

He was persecuted, even as he had persecuted others; yet he went his unfaltering way, counting it all joy to suffer for the Christ who so vividly revealed himself that day on the Damascus road— Paul the apostle, Paul the preacher, Paul the servant of the most high God, a man whose influence grows even greater with the passing of time.

37

Our heavenly Father, reveal thyself to us also, and may we, too, be wise to ask earnestly the question "Lord, what wilt thou have me to do?" And may we be wise to follow thy direction for our lives. AMEN.

The Final Triumph

There will be triumph, final and complete—
A righteous, glorious triumph when men meet
The conditions set forth by the living God.
No enemy on earth can walk roughshod
Across a land and claim a victory won
Where a people truly worship God. The sun
Would darken and the stars grow dim
Before that nation is bereft of him.

A vital, shining pentecostal day
Awaits Christ's followers on the earthly way
If they be loyal, fearless as they move
To face this troubled hour, and to prove
His infinity, his power, and his might,
To lead them out of darkness into light.

7. THE CHURCH

> Our holy and our beautiful house,
> where our fathers praised thee . . .
>
> Isa. 64:11

OUR HOLY AND OUR BEAUTIFUL HOUSE." WE READ the lovely, singing words, and we are glad for them. We truly would be a homeless people without that house! The very thought of a church brings to mind our own church, and all the other churches of the earth where needy mankind gather to worship their Lord.

What true follower of the living Christ does not love his own church membership with its sacred association? In our gladness we seek a holy shrine where we can kneel in prayer and there receive the assuring, comforting consciousness of Christ's presence. In sadness and sorrow we come to the altar, there to meet our Saviour face to face, to partake of the broken bread and the crimson wine at his dear hands, and we are sustained and strengthened thereby.

How varied are the churches of the earth! Magnificent or humble, ornate or meagerly plain, yet each one serving a holy purpose, dedicated to God.

One church in a far, backwoods place comes to mind. It is a mere shell of a building. The floor is the hard-packed earth that has been flattened by many feet throughout the years. The pews consist of logs, across which are laid roughhewn planks, with no backs against which the worshipers can rest.

One cannot but wonder how many tired people have come through all sorts of weather to sit through many services, weary, yet eager, for the earnest message that came to them from their pastor, who stood facing them behind the hand-fashioned board pulpit.

No doubt the various preachers who have occupied this pulpit throughout the years have been devout and conscientious men, or the small stipend which they received would not have held them.

These preachers knew their people well, people who probably came from far distances across the countryside to hear a message of the Christ. They knew them all, with their joys and their sorrows, their brave bearing of poverty, and their heartbreak. They knew what the seeking ones needed, and what to say to them. Always they held the Christ before their eyes—the Christ with his soul-saving power and his gracious tenderness for mankind.

Had there been no such Christ, there would be no churches upon the earth. He is the fire that warms them. He is the light that illumines them. He is the magnet that draws the millions to the open church doors, Sabbath after Sabbath, and to the midweek hour of prayer. Without his drawing power no great cathedral would stand lighted, ready to welcome its people. Without his fire no little, humble church would exist. There would

41

be but bleak, empty spaces where our churches now stand, and hearts would forever go uncomforted.

It would be strange, indeed, to come upon any town in these days where no church spire thrusts its way heavenward, like a lifted finger pointing the way that mankind should go. In a way, we of today miss much because so few bells peal forth their golden-throated call to worship.

I would like to insert a brief personal experience here. One evening at dusk I chanced to be walking down a street of a great city. I came to a cathedral that loomed magnificently in the half-light. Its doors were opened wide, and while it was not a church of my own denomination, I was drawn to enter. I sat down in a back pew. The altar candles were glimmering in the darkened interior, casting rich color and shadow on magnificent statues placed in deep niches along the walls.

One of these statues was outstanding in its artistry: a life-size figure of the Saviour on the cross, robed in crimson and purple garments. His eyes, bearing all of earth's agony, were lifted heavenward.

In the entire cathedral there was but one worshiper. She was so near me that I could see her clearly. She was beautiful and young, a girl so young one could not but wonder at such heartbreak as was seemingly hers.

She was kneeling at the feet of the crucified One, clinging with desperate hands to his nail-pierced ankles. Tears were streaming down her cheeks, and sobs were shaking her body.

I wondered what had so hurt her, what great grief had stricken her. To be sure, it was but a plaster figure to which she clung, but to her, it was the one place she knew to find the great comforter and healer of the human heart. And doubtless, back of the lifeless form, the living, breathing Christ reached down and granted new courage to her burdened heart, new comfort for her soul.

Christ is too well acquainted with all earth's sorrows to leave them unnoted. He has the healing power in his hands to aid all who come to him in prayer.

I left the cathedral after the girl had risen and gone. I had sat almost breathless lest I disturb the current of comfort I felt was flowing to her from the real Christ of all comfort, and I was grateful beyond words that we can all bring our tears to him that he may dry them, and our joys that he may share them.

"Our holy and our beautiful house." It is the fact of Christ's living presence that draws men to the house of worship. It is their love and adoration that holds them there year after year. It is their hunger for him that bids them come and be fed, their thirst for him that urges them forward to drink at the fountain of life.

It is good to think of the countless numbers of small children who have come, and are still coming, to their church schools. Sitting in their little chairs that circle their teachers, these children are learning to love Jesus—a love that will last them throughout a lifetime and on into a bright eternity.

Our Father, we thank thee for the churches of the earth with their vital meaning. We thank thee that more and more of thy children are turning back to the churches, often thronging their aisles to capacity, so great is their hunger and need for thee. We thank thee for the gift of our holy and our beautiful house. AMEN.

"The Lord Is in His Holy Temple"

Within these templed walls, the Lord is here.
He stands with outstretched arms and hands to
  greet
All who will come. The organ notes are clear,
And the voices from the choir loft are sweet.
Worship the Lord in the beauty of holiness,
Be reverent, for so many are at prayer.
Move thou along these shadowed aisles and
  bless
The earnest seeking ones who wait thee there.

O Lord God, make thy holy presence felt;
Thy touch upon the brow, Lord make it known.
Here where so many countless ones have knelt
Throughout the years, speak to each heart alone.
Lift thou the burdens weighing heavily
Upon the many, ease all wearing grief,
That there may flame a new white faith in thee:
A steadfast and unshakable belief.

> Call upon me, and I will answer thee,
> and shew thee great and mighty things,
> which thou knowest not.
>
> Jer. 33:3

H E WHO OWNS A BIBLE AND HAS THE FAITH TO accept its teachings, who heeds the gracious command to call upon a higher power than his own in any need, stands before the opened gates of breathless wonderment. He has the promise, a promise that will be kept: he will see "great and mighty things" as he enters those portals.

The majesty, the marching music, the sheer poetry of God's Word, reach deep into the human heart and prepare it for further journeying into that vast interior hitherto undiscovered. The true seeker after knowledge is certain to find it therein.

It must be a source of great joy and a mighty revelation to be privileged to carry gift Bibles into the world's darkest places, to be able to give them out freely and gladly into eager, reaching hands.

One can all but see the first steps being taken into the wonderland; the book opens in trembling hands: "In the beginning God created the heaven and the earth. . . . And God said, Let there be light: and there was light." Light beginning to dawn in the shadowed places of a mind, as well as in a new universe.

The rainbow, familiar after a storm, takes on new significance. Out under the countless stars, the voice of the great Jehovah can be heard speaking to an intent listening one. A harp's plucked strings accompany the majesty and beauty of the psalms—and always the eager expectation of the coming of the Messiah.

Then there is a sudden break among the books of this great library. There comes the vital announcement "The New Testament of our Lord and Saviour, Jesus Christ."

Here the greatest events in all history are to be unfolded for the first time to one entering those Gates of Wonder. He will enter and stand for a breathless moment beneath a molten silver star, half blinded by its brilliance. But beneath it he finds the infant Saviour and worships at his feet.

He comes into a great temple and listens to a young voice speaking with the learned doctors of the day, who are baffled by the lad's surprising knowledge of spiritual affairs.

He sees the Christ grown to manhood, ever moving with compassion among the suffering ones of earth, and he longs to fling himself at the Lord's feet for his healing power.

He is amazed and hurt at the cruelty of mankind that would send the merciful One to death on a cross. He sees him buried and, glory of glories!

47

he sees him arise from the dead! His own immortality is thus assured.

With what wonder and joy do those who have so hungered for knowledge of the Christ receive the glad tidings! What white splendors dazzle their eyes as they see him taking his way heavenward at last, leaving his followers to carry on the work he has begun! Has he not said, "Go ye into all the world, and preach the gospel to every creature"?

The recipient of that Bible knows in his heart that the giver of this wonderful gift is one of Christ's followers. Light breaks in his heart. New glory floods his soul, for the Book preaches and teaches. It is a beautiful service for our Lord to open up gates that allow all who will to enter a land of pure delight, where they can find rest and peace through the unfailing promises of God's Word.

The following poem strives to picture the absorbed interest, the wonderment and joy, of one such recipient. It is a simple telling of a true incident. Sad to relate, however, this one who had never before possessed a Bible does not live in a heathen land, but in our own country. She is one of the countless migrant workers who move from place to place, following the harvest of field or orchard and laying down no roots of stability.

The gift, left by a Christian visitor, truly opened the Gates of Wonder for this child of God. Even before the visitor had left, this woman was so absorbed in the contents of the Book that she scarcely noted his departure. Such is the power of the Word of God when it is received by an outward reaching heart, and eternity alone will tell the results.

Dear Lord, may we be among those who are following thy last command. May we, too, give out the precious gifts of thy Word to those who have no way of knowing thee hitherto. Guide us that we may fling wide the gates of knowledge so that others may have abundant proof of thy unfailing love and guidance. We ask thee in Christ's name. AMEN.

The Migrant Worker

She had never owned a Bible in her life,
This worker of the fields . . . this tired one.
The temporary camps were dull and drab
That housed her tiredness when day was done.
And then a miracle . . . a giver came
Bearing a gift: the blessed Word of God,
And gave it to the eager waiting one
There in the cabin on the rutted sod.

She sank upon her cot, the precious Book
Open in her hands, her eyes aglow . . .
Here was knowledge, here was living truth,
A thousand things that she had longed to know.
Her body tense with eagerness, she sat
Lost in a new world, lost in strange delight,
Within her hands the power to lead her through
Into the dawn, after the long, dark night.

9. GREEN PASTURES

> He is our God; and we are the people
> of his pasture.
>
> Ps. 95:7

IT IS STRANGE, YET TRUE, THAT ALL THE GREEN pastures of the Holy Word belong to us today as surely as they belonged to the people to whom the psalmist sang long ago.

We are told in the Word: "Be not afraid . . . : for the pastures of the wilderness do spring, for the tree beareth her fruit, the fig tree and the vine do yield their strength." (Joel 2:22.)

And in Job 39:8 we find that "the range of the mountains is his pasture," and "that he searcheth after every green thing."

How great are the infallible proofs of God's care over his children, his watchfulness over their welfare! What abundant pasturage is ours, and what gracious provisions are made by the great shepherd for us, his sheep!

He goes leisurely before us, bidding us feed on the lush greenness, bidding us lie down in its soft coolness when we are tired; and when we are thirsty, he leads us to the brink of clear and shining waters, where we can quench our thirst.

It must take great patience to be the good shepherd of, too often, wayward and wandering sheep. If the range of mountains is his pasture, this explains clearly how, and why, the one little bewildered lamb among the great number of others could have been lost in the rugged foothills, or even higher up on the mountainside.

It is easy to imagine the concern of the conscientious shepherd when he had safely sheltered the other sheep for the night and had found one missing. Despite earnest persuasion he went out again into the night of rain and wild wind to seek that lost one. He could not, nor would he rest, until he had found it. He came upon it at last; one can see him stooping and gently gathering the shivering creature in his arms, wrapping his cloak closely about it as he carried it back to the sheltering fold.

He had ninety and nine safely housed, but the lost one was very precious in his sight, and no effort was too great in order to save it. How like our Lord today! Each lost, straying one of us is a weight upon his heart. When he does not go personally, he bids us go find that lost one.

We see the missionaries of the world spending their last ounce of strength in search of lost souls. They work among the sick and dying; they minister to the lepers in far colonies; they feed the hungry and clothe the naked. Are they not true shepherds in Christ's kingdom? Do they not spend themselves as he spent himself that night of raging storms?

In the Word of God we come upon this statement concerning sheep and their shepherds:

Woe be unto the pastors that destroy and scatter the sheep of my pasture! saith the Lord. . . . I will gather the remnant of my flock out of all countries . . . , and will bring them again to their folds. . . . And I will set up shepherds over them which shall feed them: and they shall fear no more, nor be dismayed, neither shall they be lacking. (Jer. 23:1-4.)

Surely the earnest missionaries in all countries are the shepherds God sets up to bring the idol worshipers and the heathen-taught victims back to him and his fold.

The Lord's anger is kindled against false teachers who scatter his flock and bewilder them on the way with false doctrines and vain hopes.

Beautiful, indeed, are the pastures of the earth! The cleanest winds blow across them; there is an inherent lift of the waving grasses; there is ever a silvery light glinting across vast spaces. And there is the promise of God back of them all for his children forever.

One picture will remain in men's hearts as long as time shall last: that of a young man shepherding his father's sheep in one of the green pastures of long ago. There will be music sounding lifelong in their ears—unforgettable, soul-satisfying music.

As the sheep graze, the lad lifts the harp he is carrying, plucking on its golden strings music as clear as spring water, and as soft as impinging wings. He works for a time on his composition. Then suddenly he lift's his beautiful voice to sing the fitted words,

words that have come down through the ages, borne
on the winds of time, to hearts that have need of
their sustaining beauty and meaning:

The Lord is my shepherd; I shall not want. He
maketh me to lie down in green pastures: he leadeth
me beside the still waters. . . . Surely goodness and
mercy shall follow me all the days of my life: and I
will dwell in the house of the Lord for ever.

Gracious Father, we are grateful that we have
proof of thy abiding care that is ever over us. We
thank thee for the green pastures of the world and
for thy able shepherding. May we ever follow
closely in thy footsteps lest we go astray. In Jesus'
name we pray. AMEN.

O Gracious, Mighty Shepherd

Upon the far-flung meadowlands of earth
Thou art the shepherd, Lord. Thy clear eyes
  keep
Close watch above the little helpless ewes,
And over the often prone-to-wander sheep.
The emerald pasture compasses all lands;
Each nation is included in its reach;
All tribes and races roam that earth-wide field.
And thou art shepherd, blessed Lord, to each.

We are one world, one shepherd and one flock;
We need not fear when thou art by our side.
Make still the troubled waters of our day,
Smooth out the roughened landscape, be our
  Guide.
May thy goodness and thy mercy never cease
To lead us in the blessed ways of peace.

10. THE HOUSEHOLDS OF EARTH

> Behold, I stand at the door, and knock: if any man hear my voice, and open the door, I will come in to him, and will sup with him, and he with me.
>
> Rev. 3:20
>
> The history of the world is not in the record of great wars and conquests, but in the history of its households.
>
> —John Ruskin

WHEREVER HOUSEHOLDS ARE BEING ESTABLISHED in any land, wherever the Christ is acknowledged in the hearts of the members, early there comes a voice sounding at the door, and an insistent knocking at its panels, and blessed are they who hasten to fling the door wide to welcome that waiting Guest. He will be true to his word; he will come in and abide with them.

One of the infallible proofs of the existence of a personal Christ can be clearly observed in any Christian home. There the atmosphere is one of peace. Something of Christ's own gentleness, his thoughtfulness for others, is evidenced in the everyday living of those indwellers.

They who finally go forth from such doors definitely bear the stamp of Christ's influence. They carry with them, down the long road of memory, the consciousness of the Friend with whom they have dwelt for long. He will go with them where they go, he will stay with them where they stay, and the home they have left will stand out in their minds as a sacred place where they have been privileged to become acquainted with their gracious Lord.

There are countless young men in our government's service today. They are stationed around the world, and thus are lonely exiles from their homeland. Though not engaged in active warfare, they might be termed "standing at attention."

It is taxing work to be waiting on foreign soil for any eventuality. Temptations may befall them. Nostalgia for their homes may become intense. Perhaps there are younger brothers and sisters at home, and their hearts may ache with longing to be back with them. But blessed is that one who has been reared by a Christian father and mother in a home where there is a constant though unseen Guest sharing their days of gladness and their days of loneliness and anxiety.

That one will have stamped upon his heart such values as men die for—something permanent and worth while to which he may cling. He has a wealth of spiritual values which will stand him in good stead through times of stress and strain.

The long waiting will not seem such utter waste as he thinks of the home he knows and loves: a home where prayer is a daily rite and faith is a beautiful shining thing, a home with love and inflooding warmth that does not grow cold through the passing of the years.

Always, through the loneliness, this young man's home will glimmer before his eyes like an oasis to a thirst-driven one in a desert. It is a replica of all homes where Christ abides, and where he *must* abide if mankind is to survive. Perhaps this man will catch the light of a roof glimmering through the mist, a red chimney lifting its gray plume heavenward. There will be a garden and a flower-bordered walk, and white-curtained windows looking brightly out upon a green lawn.

As he goes home, in fancy, it will be afternoon. The door will open at the touch of his eager fingers. There will come the smell of freshly baked bread cooling on clean boards. A golden square of leaf-flecked light will glimmer on the floor. The geranium on the sill will swim in a pool of scarlet light. His mother's gingham apron will be hanging on a nearby hook, waiting her coming. The same leaking faucet will give out its sudden "plop."

There will be quietness and a sort of deep peace which belongs only to old kitchens. "Peace"—Oh, the clean, bright saneness of the word! The rest in its sound as we utter it!

The ever-abiding Guest has much to do with that peace, that established order. He has kept a father and mother serene through their days of loneliness for an absent son. He has kept them strong to go forward day by day, his hand on theirs, his everlasting arms around them. He has given them the faith that he will keep that which they have committed to his care.

And to the son this will be the assurance that, whatever comes, there will always be a Christ-companioned home waiting for him in a place of peace and light.

Thank God for homes! For any home where Christ abides. We think of it often: if our earthly home-coming after long absence brings such delight, what will our heavenly one be, with Christ's outstretched hands reaching to welcome us?

At the close of a long day, with a late light falling on land and sea, the minarets of heaven clearly in sight, why should the heart be aught but glad? Surely there will be need of rest. Surely tired shoulders should loose their load, and most certainly that journey's end should not be sad.

Some far-off evening, the last signpost past, the last corner rounded, may there be nothing but gladness in our hearts, and may we lift the same glad cry we have so often lifted upon a return to our earthly homes after long wanderings: "Home—home at last!"

Dear heavenly Father, we thank thee for thy gracious provision for our earthly needs. We thank thee for thy knock upon our doors, that thou art willing to share our simple dwelling places here upon earth; and, oh, we thank thee even more for the promise that awaits us in our eternal home. AMEN.

This Is the Book

This is the book that Martin Luther traced
With his gnarled fingers, line by precious line,
Until his probing, seeking hand unlocked
The door, and caused a radiant light to shine
Into a world that needed much that light
To illuminate the darkness of the night.

This is the book wherein John Wesley found
A pathway through the dark that all might see
A cleared and more direct way to the Christ,
A straight road leading to eternity.
He found the words that pointed out the way
To a higher plane, a brighter, happier day.

This is the book the humblest man may take
As his own map across earth's tangled sod:
Unalterable the route, unchanged by time:
A map outlined by the sure hand of God.
O pilgrims of earth, who seek a better land,
Con well that map, be guided by that hand!

11. AND NOW ABIDETH HOPE

> And now abideth faith, hope, charity;
> ... but the greatest of these is charity.
> I Cor. 13:13

IN THE GREAT SOUTHERN CITY WHERE I LIVE, A PROMInent firm has erected a signboard, a huge structure. The background is a clear pale blue that blends with our southern skies. The delicate silver scrolls that edge the board do not detract from the simple wording thereon: "And now abideth hope."

Alongside this object of beauty and artistry, distillers have lifted a liquor sign calling attention to their wares. It is brilliantly lighted, garish in color, and meant to attract the eye, but it leaves the onlooker cold.

The other sign does something to the heart. Its stark simplicity, its quiet assurance of things that abide, its spiritual significance, rest the mind and strengthen the heart.

From among the three words—faith, hope, charity—one wonders why the middle one was chosen for this particular use. Then it comes to us that our times are gravely perilous, and that hope is a great sustaining power to which we must cling in order to live at all happily and at peace—in order, in fact, to survive.

Faith, although often strong, may at times falter under stress, and charity is not always clearly evidenced; but a heart alight with hope is a gladness in the breast, without which one goes groping in darkness and desolation. This lettered board bears testimony that men of large affairs are turning to the elemental things of life—to the old simplicities.

The sign is like a clear call sounding out through the rush of traffic, the wail of sirens, all the tumult and confusion of a great city. It bids men know that despite their fears, despite the constant hammer blows of the daily headlines, despite the reports by air of present disasters, and the prophecy of evil to come, there is something that abides, and must abide, if we are to go forth to meet our days with courage and clear sight.

"And now abideth hope." How simply it is stated! It has the sound within it of Christ's own voice when he bade his distressed disciples, "Let not your heart be troubled." He told them they believed in God and he bade them to believe also in him.

His words are ever a sustaining force in the heart, and if heeded, none need be hopeless, though the future seem dark, or the present a tortuous way upon which we travel.

The ones who set up this signaling of hope no doubt had need of it in their own hearts and felt the urge to send out the message to the fearful and distraught of their community. The lettered board, with its message of cheer, is a tranquilizer more potent than the pharmacists' nostrums. We repeat the message, and it cheers and blesses us.

In studying the Bible concordance, we find that the word "hope" fills several columns—a brief word with a mighty meaning. We read: "Now the God of hope fill you with all joy and peace in believing, that ye may abound in hope, through the power of the Holy Ghost." (Rom. 5:13.) "Happy is he . . . whose hope is in the Lord." (Ps. 146:5.) "Which hope we have as an anchor of the soul, both sure and stedfast." (Heb. 6:19.) "The Lord is my portion, saith my soul; therefore will I hope in him." (Lam. 3:24.) And once David cried out: "But I will hope continually, and will yet praise thee more and more."

On and on, the word is reiterated until one becomes freshly aware of its great significance, its importance in our lives. We can, and we should, praise Jesus for that hope. Were it not for his sojourn here on earth; were it not for his life, his love, his teaching, which are as vital today as when he lived, loved, and taught among humankind—there would be no hope. But "now abideth hope," unfailing and sure for us to cling to, to move forward with, and to possess through time and eternity.

Our Lord and our God, help us to keep the white fire of hope burning in our hearts, that we may not despair, may not faint or falter upon our upward course. We pray ever in Jesus' name. AMEN.

12. THE CONQUEST OF
SORROW

He was despised and rejected of men;
a man of sorrows, and acquainted with
grief. . . . Surely he hath borne our griefs,
and carried our sorrows.

Isa. 53:3-4

BECAUSE HE HAS HITHERTO BORNE OUR GRIEF, AND
still is carrying our sorrows, should we not
strive to remember this truth and to shift
upon his strong and willing shoulders the great burdens we may be bearing, and then go our way, re-
leased and free to be about our Father's business?

If our Lord had not plumbed the depths of sorrow, and had not known intimately the most calami-
tous griefs, to whom could we go? To whom could
we turn in sorrow? Had he not gone through darkness and made his way through to the light, even
he could not understand our groping, our sense of
bewilderment, when the way seems closed ahead
and our eyes are blinded by tears.

If he had not had times of loneliness, how could
he have realized what loneliness and loss mean to
the heart? Once he said: "The foxes have holes, and
the birds of the air have nests; but the Son of man
hath not where to lay his head." Truly he must
oftentimes have been lonely.

He knew grave losses, when those he loved failed

him, denying and rejecting him. He went before us carrying a cross lifelong. He bore that cross for our sakes, that he might better be enabled to share our griefs and our sorrows, and that he could sincerely mourn with us as we mourn, and weep with us as we weep.

At the end of his earthly pilgrimage he had a most cheering word for us. He said: "I will pray the Father, and he shall give you another Comforter." He knew how desperately humanity would be needing that comfort through all the years ahead. Therefore the Holy Spirit was to come, and has come to abide in our hearts. Our part is to accept and receive him, and thus be comforted through him.

Surely he has borne our griefs and carried our sorrows. That the Christ should do this for us is breathtaking as we consider that monumental truth! He who learned what heartache means to the human race selflessly took upon himself earth's burdens, and still bears them with the help of the indwelling Holy Spirit.

The Word of God has much to say about comfort. "Comfort ye my people, saith your God. Speak ye comfortably." (Isa. 40:1-2.) We, too, should be Christlike and first travel a darkened road, if we are to "speak comfortably" to any mourning one. It would be vastly helpful through such an experience, if we could but remember that there is a purpose in the grief we are bearing and from it will come good. Something of inestimable value: an understanding sympathy for others.

To be able to go to another and say the freeing word, or even to say nothing, but by look, or a handclasp, make him know of a certainty that we understand, may bring the hurt one the healing release of tears, and new hope to his bereaved heart.

Christ was sent to a troubled world to "preach good tidings unto the meek; . . . to bind up the brokenhearted . . . ; to comfort all that mourn." We learn this from Isaiah, the great mouthpiece of God, and we have the command to comfort others.

To do so, how Christlike we should be, how much in prayer, how careful to say the right word, not one that tears a deep wound further open! We should be wise in his wisdom and strong in his strength.

In its need the heart longs for compassion. It longs to lay hold upon words of comfort, and too often it cannot find them, because we have not been about our Father's business. In the Scriptures we find this said of a mourning city: "She weepeth sore in the night, and her tears are on her cheeks: . . . she hath none to comfort her" (Lam. 1:2).

Our sympathizing helpfulness should reach out further than to the individuals. It should be city wide, world wide, in scope. Many of us cannot go personally to far lands to reach the stricken ones there, but we can help send upon errands of mercy those who are eminently fitted to be our ambassadors.

Each Christian is a link between earth and heaven. We should be strong links upon which Christ may depend to hold firm, that his purpose may be accomplished. So many do not know how to find the Christ of all comfort. It is our part to point out the road ahead, for he is on that road, our Guide who is still there in sight, if we but have eyes to see. We may be inclined to think the Almighty does not need our assistance in his eternal plan, but all through the Scriptures there is proof that he does: "Go ye . . . and teach"—"Whatsoever ye would that men should do to you, do ye even so to them"— and always, "Comfort ye my people."

In the midst of deep mourning there are often-times those who are given the Christlike power to help others, even then. I recall a remarkable Christian woman who had been bedfast for years. She had been cared for tenderly by a beloved and loving husband. One morning while he was in their garden, gathering flowers for her bedside, he died suddenly. The one who found him there was deeply grieved, but he felt a greater grief for the helpless one who was left, and he dreaded breaking the sad news to her. He feared another fatality.

But when he went to her room, she somehow knew at once the word he was bringing. The blessing of tears was denied her, but the Christ's own courage entered into her heart, and she was able to meet her sorrow bravely.

The days went by. She lived them so courageously, so bravely, that many who needed spiritual help sought her and found their hearts comforted. She had suffered, she had sorrowed, and by the grace of God she was enabled to help others.

If we have faith in the Christ of all comfort,

that faith will assure us of victory through any time of stress. Thus the conquest of sorrow can, and will, be attained.

Our heavenly Father, we thank thee that through thy Son Jesus thou hast made a way of escape from sorrow. We thank thee for sending him to earth to learn, and to teach us, thy children, how to be overcomers through thy word.

May we this day touch as many lives as possible for their good and for thy glory. In Jesus' name. AMEN.

Withheld Knowledge

One cannot know of welcoming harbor lights
Who has not braved a wild and stormy sea;
He cannot know the splendor of far heights
Who has not walked through lowlands wearily.
No one can sympathize with loneliness
If fate has cast him in a happy lot,
And he will have no healing words to bless
The one who longs for friends, and finds them
   not.

Pain is not real to one who has not trod
The roughened roads that sufferers must tread;
He cannot kneel and earnestly thank God
For sleep that is no stranger to his bed.
No traveler at all can truly value light
Who has not made his way out of the night.

13. FAITH

Now the just shall live by faith.
Heb. 10:38

OVER THE YEARS THE ABOVE TEXT HAS BEEN world-shaking. Millions have been influenced by it. It is an undeniable truth that the just do live by faith, with its sustaining power to hold the soul, mind, and body on an even keel throughout one's entire lifetime.

The true believers in the Christ as he was, and as he lives today, do not need to have the proof that was offered to Thomas, the doubting one of long ago. Our Lord does not say to them: "Reach hither thy finger, and behold my hands; and reach hither thy hand, and thrust it into my side." He asked it of Thomas, for alas! this disciple was faithless and unbelieving.

The true Christians of today have been stanch and stedfast believers lifelong, and have never had the need of physical proof of our Lord's existence, his eternal aliveness; but so great was the doubt in the heart of Thomas that he actually accepted the challenge, and he reached out and felt the wounded, outstretched palms. He ran his hand along our Lord's dear body and felt the ridges left by the inthrust sword that had wounded him.

Then, and only then, he stepped back astonished

and uttered five brief words: "My Lord and my God!" Thus he had evidence of the living presence of the Master. His words have come down through the ages to reassure any doubting one, and thus Thomas rendered a service to mankind even in his doubting.

We think of faith. We try to picture it. We cannot see it, we cannot touch it, and we do not get the answer. The King James Version tells us as nearly as it can be told: "Faith is the substance of things hoped for, the evidence of things not seen." No wonder that bungling humanity is at a loss to put the beautiful, glowing thing into words.

We know in our hearts that it is a positive force. We know that faith in the living Christ is a connecting link between us and the Eternal, and that it brings peace and rest to any troubled heart.

We realize daily its sustaining power when we fear trials and disasters or even petty annoyances that strive within us to ruin any serenity we may possess. Faith is a supply of all our needs, and it behooves us to lay hold upon it—an unseeable thing though it is. Our eyes cannot see it, our hands cannot touch it, yet it is possible to so fill our hearts with it that it cannot be lost.

Faith is a brightness and a shining way. The brave of earth have known its glory. It is a healing for long-borne hurts. It holds within it something of the silver reach of the stars. It is ever an illumination upon our pathway that guides us safely on our upward and onward way.

The observing one often witnesses faith so clear,

72

strong, unshaken, in those in whom it might seem most unlikely to exist. There are the suffering people, who through faith go forward cheerfully and bravely. There are those whose earthly lives are swiftly drawing to a close. Their faith never wavers. They look forward with joy to their heavenly homegoing, for they have faith in the warm welcome awaiting them there. There are poverty-stricken ones who are rich with an inward wealth of faith. They see the Lord's hand working for their good, even in their meager living. Their faith is truly "the substance of things hoped for."

Personally, I have been deeply impressed with the evidence of such faith shown in the lives of many a simple colored person—a faith that makes their dark faces glow with light. Often they put many professed Christians of another race to shame for their lack of trust, their absence of true faith in their heavenly Father.

There is one case I recall which proves what faith, "the unseen evidence," can do. The old servant in the household had to have the news imparted to her of the sudden death of an especially beloved brother. She had lost all the other members of her family, and now the last one was gone.

The mistress of the household had feared to tell her the word that had come by telephone, for the servant was old and rather feeble, but she stood up under the shock like a true soldier. Through her tears she exclaimed: "The Lord he give, and the Lord he take away. Blessed be the dear Lord's name."

The mistress told her that she felt she was very brave, and this was her answer: "You know, Missy, if I is brave it is 'cause I is like what St. Paul he say in our Bible, he say: 'I live by faith of the son of God who loved us enough to given his life for us, dat's why.'" And there was no further need of fear that the good woman would break beneath the blow of the sudden shock.

The dear soul had so steeped her being in the word of God that she had the answer for every time of need. She lived "by faith of the Son of God." She had the infallible proof of his saving power, and in that faith we, too, should live.

Heavenly Father, may we become so familiar with thy Word, and with thy purpose in our lives, that we, too, may know its answer to all of life's perplexities and its sorrows and its woes. Help us to move forward upon a pathway lighted by faith in thy Son Jesus Christ, in whose name we pray. AMEN.

That by Which We Live

It is not bread alone by which we live;
It is not sight or touch or breath that keeps
The steady heartbeats pulsing in our breast,
Nor is it rest that comes to him who sleeps.
That by which we live is something more:
A vital and life-giving force that stays
Our heart, our hands, our feet—a force that
    gives
Us power to walk uprightly through our days.

Men call it faith—a substance yet unseen,
Impenetrable armor that we wear,
A shield held firm against the fiery darts
That evil may unloose upon the air.
It is a thing of splendor, a clear light
By which we travel safely day or night.

14. HARMONY

> That they all may be one; as thou,
> Father, art in me, and I in thee, that they
> also may be one in us: that the world
> may believe that thou hast sent me. And
> the glory which thou gavest me I have
> given them; that they may be one, even
> as we are one.
>
> John 17:21-22

THIS IS OUR DEAR LORD'S PRAYER FOR THE CHURCH, and for all who would believe on him through the words of the apostles, and through the preaching of those who were to succeed them throughout the generations to come. It is proof of his grave concern for us his people.

It is a prayer that covers the peoples of all nations, and it was uttered as he was moving steadily forward on the road to Calvary. Even then he took the time to speak out in behalf of the human race, forgetting himself and his suffering to come, in his great desire for the good of mankind.

His prayer was ever for others. His desire for his children is that we may be one with him and his Father, a united family living in unity and peace in the world. His longing for us is that we as Christians will so live "that the world may believe." He wants this harmony felt by others. He wants its influence to draw the world into that beautiful fellowship. He would have us be one in spirit, one in rights and privileges, and one as future inhabitants of the world to come.

The lack of peace on earth today, the lack of accord among nations, the fear and unrest in the hearts of mankind, must grieve him unutterably. We know that such a lack exists because his words, so earnestly spoken in our behalf, go unheeded, and heart-warming prayer has thus been unanswered.

Surely the years are passing all too swiftly away, and it is time that our hearts should be "tuned to the infinite," that we may receive the greatest possible blessing for which Christ prayed that far-off day.

He prayed for peace, harmony, love, and at last for eternal glory for us all. This can come only by making ourselves one with him and obedient to his will: one as he and the Father are one. It can be done, or he would not have prayed for it.

How can we achieve that perfect harmony, that unity? It can be accomplished only by working together through love for each other and by following the divine leadership, the great director of our human destinies; and out of that harmony will come the celestial music of eternity.

The love of harmony is demonstrated daily in nature: the silent turning of the earth through space, the quiet moving of the stars in their courses, the seasons' inevitable coming and going, bespeak God's love of order and harmony.

We all have heard the tuning up of a great orchestra: a shriek here, a rasp there, the discordant plucking of strings, the jangle of falsely struck keys—all the din of chaos as the musicians ready themselves and their instruments for an important performance.

One wonders what music could possibly come from that wild tumult, and then, the master appears: the chairs are in order, the instruments in place, the baton is lifted, and out of the distracting welter of discords comes a burst of music in perfect harmony, the instruments in exact tune.

The violins sing out, the golden trumpet notes climb to the ceiling, the trombones give forth their silvery tones, all in an exquisite harmony of sound that lifts outward and upward, climbing, it seems, to the very gates of heaven. The musicians, their eyes upon him, are following the master, his hands their hands, his movements their movements, "that they may all be one."

God grant that in the great symphony of life we may follow closely the directing of our Master, and thus help to answer our Lord's most beautiful prayer. How wonderful, how marvelous, to be associated with the creator of the universe, in tune with him—his glory our glory, his peace our peace, his will our will!

True, we cannot all be great musicians, but we can, as we follow our Master's leading, become one with him, moving as he moves, resting as he rests —for the rest in the compositions of life are quite

as important as the spirited swinging movements—
and thus a glorious whole can, and will, be sustained.

We should be one with our Lord in his great love
for humanity, one with him in the pursuit of peace
with all nations, one with him in charity when there
is need, and one with him in long-suffering, if we
are to learn his patience and trust in the will and
wisdom of his Father.

"I am the vine, ye are the branches." (John 15:
5.) Could any objects be more closely allied? The
same roots feed the main stalk that feed the frail
offshoots. The blood in the veins of leaf and flower
is the lifeblood from the root. The output of fruit
belongs to the whole of creation. We should be
grateful to be sharers with Christ in that upward
climb, that sharing of the ultimate fruit.

God gives us each a place to fill, a task to do. He
wants us to harmonize in the world's work. Oh, may
we keep the instruments of our lives, our minds, ever
in tune with his!

Our Lord, help us to tune our hearts so accurately
with thine that there may be no discord in the
music of our living. We would be one with thee,
ready to heed thy bidding, eager to follow thy di-
rections. Help us to keep our eyes so fixed on thee
that our part in the orchestra of life may not mar
the perfect whole. In Jesus' name we ask it. AMEN.

15: SHARED POWER

> Now Peter and John went up together
> into the temple at the hour of prayer,
> being the ninth hour. And a certain man
> lame from his mother's womb was
> carried, whom they laid daily at the gate
> of the temple which is called Beautiful,
> to ask alms of them that entered into
> the temple.
>
> Acts 3:1-2

THERE ARE CERTAIN PASSAGES IN OUR BIBLE THAT especially rejoice the heart. It is good to read of the marvelous miracles performed by the Master, and always we are made glad by the accounts of joy shown by some fortunate one who, at Christ's touch, was restored to sudden radiant health.

This same Christ still is mindful of the suffering ones of earth. One of the many proofs of his continued care is that he shared his healing power with his disciples, bidding them to go forth and heal the sick and to meet every human need.

We can see the ones who daily brought a young man, crippled from his birth, and laid him down before the Beautiful Gate, where he would ask for alms continually of those who entered the temple.

It was a good place for that purpose, since most of those who came had coins for various contributions that were bound to be solicited in the temple, and many hearts must have been touched by the pitiful condition of this helpless man.

We read of the gates that opened into the temple —nine in all. Eight of them were of the same size, ornamented with gold and silver plating and lovely to look upon. But the gate called Beautiful far surpassed the others. Enormous in size, it opened directly off Solomon's porch and was the gate entered most often. Apparently it was wrought from Corinthian brass, and was inlaid with solid gold and silver designs in bas-relief. It was kept burnished and bright, and it was evidently greatly admired by the throngs that sought the temple at the hour of prayer.

The prayer services were usually held morning, noon, and night, but on this special occasion it was the ninth hour, which evidently was three o'clock in the afternoon. The poor beggar had lain in one position, and in one place, since early morning. How weary he must have been, and how disheartened! Then he observed two men about to enter the temple. They were strangers to him, but, unknown to him, they were the Christ's own ambassadors of good will—Peter and John. Surely the Christ had guided them to the temple at this particular hour, for his power was immediately manifested.

At the call for alms the two stopped suddenly, and Peter, his burning zealot eyes fixed on the man, bade him look at them. Of course, this command was obeyed, for the impotent one was certain he was about to receive the requested alms, but instead, Peter spoke to him: "Silver and gold have I none; but such as I have give I thee: In the name of Jesus Christ of Nazareth rise up and walk."

Then Peter took the man by his right hand and lifted him up. And wonder of wonders! the withered feet and ankles received strength, and the man stood upright. He walked slowly—a step, two steps—and then he began leaping and praising God, shouting aloud in his great exultation and joy.

The people, hearing the unusual tumult, gathered hurriedly to note the cause. They saw the one whom they were accustomed to see lying helpless beside the Beautiful Gate, but now he was leaping and rejoicing, giving God the glory, and they were speechless with wonder. Here before their eyes were being fulfilled, in the most literal manner, the words of the prophet Isaiah: "Then shall the lame man leap as an hart."

As the crowds continued to gather, Peter asked them why they marveled so at this, and why they looked on John and him as though by their power or holiness they had made this man whole. He went on to say:

The God of Abraham, and of Isaac, and of Jacob, the God of our fathers, hath glorified his Son Jesus; whom ye delivered up, and denied him in the presence of Pilate . . . ; and killed the Prince of life, whom God hath raised from the dead; whereof we are witnesses.

And his name through faith in his name hath made this man strong, whom ye see and know.

A new, bolder Peter, under the influence of the Holy Spirit, missed no opportunity to testify for his Lord. He wisely led up to the Christ whom they had denied—first by speaking of the One they called their God, showing that God had acknowledged Jesus Christ as his Son, and that this miracle was performed in the Son's name.

The scripture goes on to say: "Now when they saw the boldness of Peter and John, and perceived that they were unlearned and ignorant men, . . . they took knowledge of them, that they had been with Jesus."

It seems that none of the apostles could have been entirely "unlearned" and "ignorant" in the usual acceptation of the terms, for had not Jesus chosen them from among many as men of intelligence and foresight? True, they may not have followed literary pursuits, but had they not been with Jesus, the master teacher of all time, and had they not, through obedience to his word, learned many invaluable truths?

There by the Beautiful Gate, where an outstanding miracle had been performed in the name of the living Christ, men who hitherto had been unbelievers saw this power transferred, in part, to others, saw that the men who had been closely associated with him possessed something they lacked; and then and there "they took knowledge of them, that they had been with Jesus."

Perhaps the transformation in the onlookers' hearts that day was, in its way, as great as that which had taken place in the life of the crippled man.

Would it not behoove us to be so closely allied with our Lord and his work that men beholding us would see the Christ reflected clearly in our lives? He has commanded us to go about doing good in his name. Shall we not heed his counsel? Shall we, too, not share in his power?

Our Lord and our God, we believe that every true follower of thy dear Son shares in his desire and in his ability to help the crying needs of our time. Grant that we may be transmitters of thy power, and we will ever give the glory to the One in whose name we pray. AMEN.

The Master Teacher

Through these unquiet years of vague unrest
It is time for many a conference with the Christ
Who is supreme as teacher and as friend,
Whose life on earth was early sacrificed,
And yet he lives today with vital power:
Clear-eyed and simply and direct he speaks,
Unquestionable his judgments, wise his words,
And unfailing is his love for him who seeks.

O Master Teacher, we would cultivate
Thy intellectual sanity and strength,
And through communion with thee, blessed
    Lord,
We can meet the years, no matter what their
    length,
Consulting, heeding, trusting thee to give
The knowledge which we need by which to live.

16. WITNESSING

Ye are my witnesses, saith the Lord.
Isa. 43:10

A S CHRISTIANS WE ARE ON THE WITNESS STAND
every hour of every day. We must know
what is the truth and bear witness to that
truth.

We must know intimately our risen Lord, and this
it is possible to do, for has he not called us friends?
We must hide his Word in our hearts that we may
not sin against him. We must offer our praise
clearly and convincingly, so that others may know
of the divine companionship we have with our
Lord. We must speak out so sincerely, so truthfully,
that the jury of the world before which we stand
may know we are faithful witnesses for our Lord and
Saviour, Jesus Christ.

How often we should praise him with words so
warm and loving, and so positive that they will
become an impelling, drawing power to others!

Christ himself still stands before the tribunals
of the world—a world ready to condemn him today as it did long ago. We must be his stanch
advocates and his followers.

We stand as his witnesses, and, with his help,
many an onlooker, faltering between two opinions,

may be led to favor the Lord through our activities and the words we speak in his behalf.

Since we are thus important in his eternal scheme, is it not strange that we are so often alert, so active on our feet, as we go about our business of living, and that we are so seldom upon our knees in order that we may know more about the Lord and his vast eternal affairs?

He tells us to "be still, and know." He wants us to stay close to him until he can teach us the intricacies of the work of his kingdom. Only through tarrying before him can we testify gloriously to his grace, his mercy, and his power to save. Only then can our words ring true to our fellow men, and we will forget to glorify ourselves and will glorify him—our Father who is in heaven.

We are his witnesses. No greater honor, no greater responsibility, was ever bestowed upon mankind than this—to be Christ's own devoted followers. May we strive earnestly to be faithful to that trust.

In Jer. 50:5 we find these words: "They shall ask the way to Zion with their faces thitherward, saying, Come, and let us join ourselves to the Lord in a perpetual covenant."

Not only should individuals be stanch witnesses for our Lord, but never before has our nation so needed to walk uprightly, and to be a true example of Christianity to the other nations of the world, as it does today.

We should set our faces toward the high goal of righteousness and not waver in the journey. This should be a day of strict obedience to the law, and the will, of God. We should inquire earnestly the way, and walk therein, never faltering. There is a perilous journey ahead, and we as a people should not attempt to travel it alone.

"Come, and let us join ourselves to the Lord in a perpetual covenant that shall not be forgotten." The word "perpetual" is a vital, a strong word. It is good to think of it in connection with the Lord, his will, and his work. It is blessed to think of his perpetual care, his perpetual saving power, his perpetual love that will not let us go if we but trust him. Oh, that our nation would be an outstanding witness for Jesus Christ! Oh, that those who observe us might take notice of our uprightness in our dealings, our justice to all!

Why should we not be perpetual in our faith, our obedience, and our devotion to him? When we make that covenant, then, and then only, shall we be marching forward to victory and peace. "Ye are my witnesses." That goal is not impossible of attainment! The Guide awaits. Let us move forward with hope in our hearts, sustained by the knowledge of a covenant between us and our never-failing Lord, a covenant not to be forgotten.

In closing may we pray the prayer of Francis of Assisi:

Lord, make me an instrument of your peace; where there is hatred, let me sow love; where there is injury, pardon; where there is doubt, faith; where there is despair, hope; where there is darkness, light; and where there is sadness, joy.

O Divine Master, grant that I may not so much seek to be consoled as to console; to be understood, as to understand; to be loved, as to love; for it is in giving that we receive, it is in pardoning that we are pardoned, and it is in dying that we are born to eternal life. AMEN.

17. PRAYER POWER

> The effectual fervent prayer of a right-
> eous man availeth much.
>
> Jas. 5:16

O H, THE BLESSED PRIVILEGE OF PRAYER: THE
wonder of it that the Almighty, with his
hands steadying a universe of sun and moon
and stars, should take the time and should be willing to lend an attentive ear to the voices of his
earthly children!

We scan the above text and are conscious of its
truth. Truly a good man's prayer "availeth much";
but we also know that the petition of a good woman and that of a little innocent child have that same
all-prevailing power, as their prayers like white
flames lift upward to God.

We are told that "all flesh [shall] come to worship before me." The most evil one, the worst
derelict, will in time come to the God he may
have denied lifelong.

No intercession is ignored by our Lord, and there
is no moment, day or night, when prayer is not
ascending from the hearts and lips of mankind.
For so great is the need, so mighty the desire, to
contact a power higher than our own, that humanity truly prays without ceasing, as the Bible has
bidden us do. It is amazing to think of the various

prayers that are arising constantly to knock at the gates of heaven and to beat against the breast of our Lord.

There are the weary, importuning him for rest; there are the suffering ones, crying out in agony for relief; and, oh, there are the countless rejoicing ones, lifting up their voices in praise for answered prayer. Their expressed joy must be like celestial music in our Lord's ears, and how especially pleased he must be for the gratitude that has not been withheld!

While these prayers are ascending, so few wait for the answering voice that is certain to come, if we but be quiet and listen. He has told us, "Be still and know that I am God." Surely we can still our clamoring tongues at this reasonable request from One who is willing to give considered attention to our petitions.

Prayer is power. What miracles it has wrought! There are few earnest praying Christians who cannot testify to the wonder and the glory of answered prayer.

There are many infallible proofs given to us by our Lord, who bade us pray, and who, in his simple, beautiful language, taught us how to pray. There is ever the consciousness of a divine presence in our hearts as we sense his nearness and turn to him in prayer, without which we would go stumbling blindly along the rugged road of life, disheartened and discouraged.

Our God is an unfailing fountainhead of blessings and mercies for all who will tap his spring of living water. May we, in our need, come often to that thirst-quenching source. We have his promise that our need will be supplied.

True, he does not always answer our prayers as we may desire, but instead he has promised "some better thing": something far better for our ultimate good than that for which we have prayed.

We have proof of this in God's own Word: "And these all, having obtained a good report through faith, received not the promise: God having provided some better thing for us" (Heb. 11: 39-40).

Personally, looking back, I can recall that I have often prayed wild, clamoring prayers that must have sounded loud in the ears of our Lord— prayers no father would be wise to grant his child. My life would have been a shambles had those pleadings been answered according to my desires, and so I have come to thank God for unanswered prayer.

What unutterable confusion would result if every prayer of God's children were granted! How fortunate we are that there is a strong, steadying hand not only upon the universe, but upon our individual lives! How wise is his guidance!

This I know, our heavenly Father always answers prayer in one way or another. If he sees that granting our prayer will be for our good, his answer is yes; if not, it will be no, and rightly so. We can trust his will and his perfect judgment.

If we accept his will, if we bow to it and await the outcome through any dark experience, I believe he accepts our attitude as the highest form of worship, and our prayers will then "be set forth before [him] as incense; and the lifting up of [our] hands as the evening sacrifice."

Prayer is power—Oh, let us pray!

Dear heavenly Father, we come to thee often at thy bidding. Too many times we ask amiss. Forgive our faulty human utterances, and make us worthy of thy blessed consideration and attention. We would pray according to thy will. In Jesus' name we ask it. AMEN.

Lay Hold of Power

Lay hold on it, O hearts, lay hold of Power
So great that heaven and earth stand still to see
Its working force. As you contact your God,
The current he releases will set free
A light across the darkest, deepest night,
And strength for any heavy burdening load:
There will be mercy in that unloosed Power
And courage for the steepest, roughest road.

Reach out in faith and touch that Inner Spring:
The voltage set in motion will not fail.
The Powerhouse of heaven works for you.
Your earnest prayers sent upward will prevail.
Lay hold, O hearts, upon that Power and find
New strength of body, and deep peace of mind.

18. THE ILLUMINATING
CHRIST

> I will speak of the glorious honour of
> thy majesty, and of thy wondrous works.
> Ps. 145:5

THUS SPAKE DAVID THE PSALMIST, AND THUS should we speak.

Today as we meet one another, singly or in groups, why do we not more often speak freely of God, our heavenly Father; of Jesus, our mutual, compassionate friend; and of the Holy Spirit, our abiding guide and comforter?

David also says: "One generation shall praise thy works to another." Have those of past generations failed in this important matter of enlightenment and praise of our God? Of what do we speak today as we meet? Is it not of the weather, of a current political scandal, of the latest fashion, of the day's amusement—inconsequential, ephemeral things that blow across our minds like turbulent winds, leaving nothing of value in their passing?

We read in Malachi that the ones who feared the Lord—those who loved and honored him—spoke often of him one to another, and so pleased was he that this was so, a book of remembrance was written before him, and those who thought upon his name were marked to be his precious jewels later on. It would be marvelous to be thus chosen and thus honored. That choice and that honor can be unfailingly ours also, if we strive to be worthy to claim them.

Alas, too often we are dullards. We are not luminous in our Lord's sight as we should be. We miss the glory that should be ours through lack of continuous contact with him.

We could be like an especially beautiful cathedral window which I have in mind, but too often we are like it only on those occasions when it is shrouded in darkness. In the shadows it is but a somber grayness set in a massive wall.

However, when the sun shines brightly, this somber window becomes a gorgeous mosaic of color, like so many jewels blazing with light. And in the midst of the radiance is portrayed the Christ ascending heavenward, his hands reaching out to bless all who will receive his blessing—all who will let his light shine through them to illuminate their beings and to reach out gloriously to others.

So brilliant is that jeweled figure, that one all but closes one's eyes to fully catch its blinding beauty. We need the light of the Christ. We need his glory shining through us to make us a drawing power. We should have him as our central, moving force, and we should become strong magnets that will draw others to him.

Again Malachi speaks (4:2), "But unto you that fear my name shall the Sun of righteousness arise with healing in his wings." How like the lovely window of which we are thinking! The sun of his righteousness will shine through us, will permeate our beings as he rises before us, offering us the healing of forgiveness and salvation as he takes his upward way; and his blessing will rest graciously upon us.

How marvelously he does his part! How mindful we should be to do ours—to glorify him, to honor him, and to speak often one to another of his mighty works, his majesty, and his honor!

What blessed testimonies our fathers and mothers once voiced in the midweek prayer services! Has it become old-fashioned to do so now? Or are there no radiant experiences to relate? Is it thought of as overemotional for some saved and sanctified soul to shout his joy aloud in meeting?

I recall a gracious, gentle elderly woman who, in her everyday life, was as meek and quiet as a gray-winged dove. Suddenly one evening at the altar she became so joyously happy, so eager to express her love and adoration for Christ's saving power, that she arose from her knees and all but floated on the air as she moved forward and backward across the rostrum, crying out her praises in a gentle yet penetrating voice.

It was a memorable experience to witness the moving of the Holy Spirit in that dear soul as she lifted her voice in gratitude and praise of One altogether lovely. I assure you that all those who saw the evidence of adoration for our Lord thus expressed, had nothing but reverence in their hearts for her, the saintly one, giving voice to a compelling inward power. It was a striking testimony of faith in a living Christ.

Oh, may we speak often one to another of our Lord! Let us not make him a stranger in our midst, but rather may we behold him as a companion and a friend—One beloved greatly—and may we do nothing ever to block his light from our lives.

Heavenly Father, we would be mindful of thy mighty words, thy majesty, and thy honor. Forgive us for our seeming indifference of them, and of thy vital meaning in our lives. Open wide thy book of remembrance, and may our names be worthy to be there inscribed by thy gracious hand. We ask it in Jesus' name. AMEN.

Church Spires

I never see a church's spire
But I am prone to wonder
At its vast reach, as high and higher
It rends the air asunder:
A lifted cry for God to note
Man's recognition of him.
It is as if deft fingers wrote
With words to say they love him.

A church spire tipped with a white star,
And jeweled by its splendor,
Is lovely as it reaches far
To strive to pierce the slender
Crescent of a moon swung high . . .
Each upward climbing steeple
Is worship flung against the sky
By God's devoted people.
Oh, may more spires lift from the sod
To please the watching eyes of God.

19. CLEAR SHINING AFTER RAIN

> So the Lord blessed the latter end of
> Job more than his beginning.
>
> Job 42:12

CLEAR SHINING AFTER RAIN!" THESE BEAUTIFUL
words are quoted from an old hymn written
by William Cowper long years ago. They
are included in the stanza that follows:

> Sometimes a light surprises
> The Christian while he sings;
> It is the Lord who rises
> With healing in His wings.
> When comforts are declining
> He grants the soul again
> A season of clear shining,
> To cheer it after rain.

Here is one who suffered much, who bore that
suffering with admirable fortitude, and then suddenly the Lord would come "with healing in his
wings" and bring blessed relief.

This would be the light he speaks of in the
hymn's first line—a surprising, an all-pervading
light—and his soul would be granted again "a
season of clear shining" that flooded his entire
being with radiance as sunlight floods the earth

with golden glory after a long, dark, tempestuous day.

William Cowper's life was an extremely solitary one. He was forced to be much alone, and he was considered by his farmer neighbors as being odd and eccentric. His life seemed to them to be valueless, since only physical labor appealed to them as being worth while.

However, the names of those good farmers are long since forgotten, while the personality of William Cowper remains as something shining and of lasting charm. The way he battled continually against distress and weakness; his determination to be kind and gentle and happy despite grave personal difficulties; and the whiteness of his soul as revealed in his letters, his poetry, and his hymns —all combine to give the name of William Cowper a luster and a quiet strength that endures.

Here is one who kept waiting through long periods of distress for that clear shining to break forth, but out of his suffering came greatness. It is often thus. Greatness does not grow in shallow soil: it must develop slowly before it springs from the dark depths of one's being. The soil must be enriched by patience and watered with tears. It must, and will be, watched over by the all-seeing God, the gardener of life. He it is who finally gives the soul an upward lift into the light, "to cheer it" after discouragement and grief.

No healing comes to anyone unless this same

Jesus who walked the earth, and who healed each sufferer he met, does the healing. It is through divine power that all good comes to mankind. One can be assured that as pain lifts, whether soon or late, God's hand has done the lifting. The endeavor to rise above the darkness may be the task of the individual, but God is in that struggle with him. He is helping to break the stubborn sod, that there may be the surprising light that comes when the sod is fully broken.

If it is God's will that one be lifted up for fuller service in this life, or if it be otherwise, and death releases one from suffering, it will be no less a lifting, no less a lasting clear shining after darkness.

One who, through grave difficulties, has been bravely trusting and patiently waiting for the working of a higher power will then be freed from all life's hurts and loosed to joyously climb the glittering hills of heaven, unencumbered. For truly then the Lord has arrived with "healing in his wings."

We go back to our text, where we find words of cheer and encouragement for any heart bowed down with pain or sorrow. No one ever had borne greater affliction than did Job. It looked impossible for him to come through to better days after the darkness of his long night.

He was stripped of all his possessions; he was horribly hurt in body and spirit; he was human enough to wonder at the grievous things that had befallen him. His was the struggle, surely, yet in his anguish he cried out in one of the bravest

102

utterances ever made by mankind: "Let come on me what will. . . . Though he slay me, yet will I trust in him." And God heard his cry and worked for the healing, which came in a glorious way.

There came to Job a "clear shining" after the raging storm—a blinding light after darkness—which truly must have surprised him. One wonders how many long-suffering ones have conned the book of Job and have found new courage, new hope, and new strength in the fact of the Lord's blessing the latter days of Job even "more than the beginning." The beginning had been marvelous in itself, but, after all Job had endured, to receive greater blessings, greater renewal of body and of spirit, this, to many, must be a revelation of the healing power of the Lord.

There are countless ones today who go about bearing pain patiently and bravely. Sometimes that pain is mercifully lifted, but these people may not, among the multitude of fellow mortals, be conscious of having met the Master on the way. However, it was Jesus whose hand lifted their pain. It was no less a miracle than that upon the road to Jericho: no less than that of the blind man who received his sight beneath the touch of Jesus' healing fingers. No less their hearts leaped with joy than did the hearts of those to whom the Master revealed himself in person.

There is daily proof of his presence, if we but watch for those proofs and give him credit and praise for his mighty works among us. May we ever be mindful of him and of his power in our lives.

Dear Lord, the world's hurts are grievous today. We pray thee, walk down the streets and the byways of the earth, go into the nursing homes everywhere, and touch with thy healing hands all those who are bravely bearing heavy burdens of grief and suffering. Make them rejoice in the clear shining of thy presence. We ask it in Jesus' name. AMEN.

I Heard the World at Prayer

I heard the world at prayer—I heard the plead-
    ing
Of countless souls whose voices do not cease:
The urgent and insistent prayer of nations
Crying out for universal peace.

I heard the pastors of great churches praying
With God for a revival in our time,
Their earnest, sincere utterances lifting
Like incense in its upward reaching climb.

I heard a strong man praying for forgiveness,
I heard a woman weighted down with care
Cry out to God. Oh, I have heard earth's an-
    guish
Made vocal in an agony of prayer.

And I have seen the gladness when the answer
Has come with mercy from the throne of God,
With full assurance that his peace is granted,
That man may walk light-hearted on earth's
    sod.

And there will be a great and sure revival
When mankind pray together in their need.
God, God, we lift a hallelujah chorus
For answered prayer. We praise thee, Lord,
    indeed.

20. THE PATHWAY OF LIFE

> Thou wilt shew me the path of life:
> in thy presence is fulness of joy; at thy
> right hand there are pleasures for ever-
> more.
>
> Ps. 16:11

WE HAVE HOURLY, DAILY PROOFS OF CHRIST'S abiding presence in our lives. Our pathways are lighted by the assurance of his love and care. They are strewn with his rich mercies and blessings.

We have the hope given us, and we should have the unfaltering faith that all eternity ahead is filled with a brightness that our holden eyes cannot now see, nor can our ears hear—they are not yet equipped to catch the celestial music of eternity.

Truly, as we have been told: "Eye hath not seen, nor ear heard, neither have entered into the heart of man, the things which God hath prepared for them that love him" (I Cor. 2:9).

We should more often be conscious of Christ's presence here and now. We pray, and he is beside us, attentive and listening to our cries. We suffer, and he suffers with us. We rejoice, and he is made glad.

There may be times when the bright pathway seems to grow dark before our eyes. The road ahead may appear to be closed, and we become fearful that we cannot go forward; but suddenly, he sheds a light upon our way and we can follow it fearlessly, sensing his presence and his accurate guidance.

Often we may feel that it would be blessed and glorious if we could but see the living and breathing Christ at our side as we journey; but we walk by faith and not by sight, and faith itself is an illumination within our inner beings. Our Lord's presence is no less real because our eyes cannot see his form, his face. He wants us to trust that he is close beside us and to move forward in accordance with his will concerning us.

Also the psalmist David cried from a full heart: "Hold up my goings in thy paths, that my footsteps slip not. I have called upon thee, for thou wilt hear me." (Ps. 17:5-6.)

Again he exclaims: "Thou art near, O Lord; and all thy commandments are true." How certain was David of that Comrade by his side! He did not doubt that any call he might make on his close Friend would fail to be heard and answered in a way that was right and best.

Following his resurrection and his brief stay upon the earth, Christ knew how vitally important it was, and still is today, for his followers to be conscious of his presence in the daily walks of life. He wants us to feel him so near that we may never lose the sense of that blessed nearness.

We believe that often he longs for us, in times of need, to stretch forth a hand of faith and touch his garments, even as did the earnest seeking one of old. Can we not well believe that his virtue can and will flow to us as it did to the suffering one that far-off day?

We know that he is more than willing to abide with us under our own rooftree and that he stays with us during the long watches of the night. We are assured that this is so. Why should we not take it literally?

Christ himself gave us the full assurance of his abiding presence when he said: "Lo, I am with you alway even unto the end of the world." And again, he uttered these comforting words: "I will never leave thee, nor forsake thee." After these forthright and beautiful statements should we not take heart and go hopefully forward on our earthly pilgrimage?

We think of the countless thousands who have clung to the following promise: "Fear thou not; for I am with thee : be not dismayed; for I am thy God: I will strengthen thee; yea, I will help thee; yea, I will uphold thee with the right hand of my righteousness" (Isa. 41:10).

And then later there comes the further assurance: "For I the Lord thy God will hold thy right hand, saying unto thee, Fear not; I will help thee."

One can picture the loving Christ reaching down to take the hand of some bewildered, fearful one, thereby lending him the strength needed for the upward climb. What a beautiful companionship is ours if we but accept it!

He says over and over, "Fear thou not; for I am with thee." He reinforces his statement: "Be strong and of a good courage, fear not . . . : for the Lord thy God, he it is that doth go with thee; he will not fail thee, nor forsake thee" (Deut. 31:6).

God grant that we may depend more fully upon his gracious promises! Should we not walk the earth with quiet dignity and with a righteous pride, for are we not close akin to royalty? Are we not the children of a great, ever-reigning King?

Our dear Lord, may we ever be conscious of the illumination that thy presence sheds upon our pathways. Help us to walk courageously because thou art with us, guiding and directing us toward thy kingdom which is in heaven. AMEN.

"Let There Be Light"

"And God said, Let there be light: and there
  was light."
From the morning of creation there was lit
A steady flame by the mighty hand of God,
Who looked upon his work, and valued it.
"He saw that it was good," and later lights
Shone through his Word for the guidance of
  mankind,
That none need lose his way out through the
  night,
That none need falter though his eyes be blind:

An all-pervading light that we may go
Free and unhindered on our heavenward way.
Men call the latter light "God's holy Word,"
He called the first illumination "Day."
We have his Word, a light that does not dim,
And his Day in which to make our way to him.